GOD'S GREATEST BIBLE PROMISES

FOR

COMFORT IN DIFFICULT TIMES

WHITAKER
HOUSE

God's Greatest Bible Promises for Comfort in Difficult Times
Over 100 Scriptures from the King James Version Easy Read Bible (KJVER)

ISBN: 979-8-88769-334-7
eBook ISBN: 979-8-88769-335-4
Printed in the United States of America

Whitaker House
1030 Hunt Valley Circle New Kensington, PA 15068
www.whitakerhouse.com

Library of Congress Control Number: 2024922503

1 2 3 4 5 6 7 8 9 10 31 30 29 28 27 26 25

CONTENTS

GOD'S PROMISES WHEN YOU FEEL...

AFRAID

For I the Lord your God will hold your right hand, saying to you, Fear not; I will help you.

—Isaiah 41:13

What time I am afraid, I will trust in You. In God I will praise His word, in God I have put my trust; I will not fear what flesh can do to me.

—Psalm 56:3–4

The LORD is my light and my salvation;
whom shall I fear?
the LORD is the strength of my life;
of whom shall I be afraid?
—Psalm 27:1

He shall cover you with His feathers, and under His wings shall you trust: His truth shall be your shield and buckler. You shall not be afraid for the terror by night; nor for the arrow that flies by day; nor for the pestilence that walks in darkness; nor for the destruction that wastes at noonday.

—Psalm 91:4–6

Fear not: for I have redeemed you,
I have called you by your name;
you are Mine.

—Isaiah 43:1

Fear you not; for I am with you: be not dismayed; for I am your God: I will strengthen you; yea, I will help you; yea, I will uphold you with the right hand of My righteousness.

—Isaiah 41:10

God has not given us the spirit of fear;

but of power, and of love,

and of a sound mind.

—2 Timothy 1:7

BROKENHEARTED

The Lord is near to them that

are of a broken heart;

and saves such as be of a contrite spirit.

—Psalm 34:18

Let not your heart be troubled:
you believe in God, believe also in Me.
—John 14:1

Praise you the Lord....
He heals the broken in heart,
and binds up their wounds.
—Psalm 147:1, 3

Weeping may endure for a night, but joy comes in the morning.

—Psalm 30:5

You tell my wanderings:
put You my tears into Your bottle: are
they not in Your book?...
This I know; for God is for me.
In God will I praise His word: in the
Lord will I praise His word.
—Psalm 56:8–10

BURDENED

Come to Me, all you that labor and are heavy laden, and I will give you rest. Take My yoke upon you, and learn of Me; for I am meek and lowly in heart: and you shall find rest to your souls. For My yoke is easy, and My burden is light.

—Matthew 11:28–30

The LORD raises them that

are bowed down.

—Psalm 146:8

Stand fast therefore in the liberty wherewith Christ has made us free, and be not entangled again with the yoke of bondage.

—Galatians 5:1

Cast your burden upon the LORD,
and He shall sustain you: He shall never
allow the righteous to be moved.
—Psalm 55:22

For You have broken the yoke of his burden, and the staff of his shoulder, the rod of his oppressor.... For to us a Child is born, to us a Son is given: and the government shall be upon His shoulder: and His name shall be called Wonderful, Counselor, The Mighty God, The Everlasting Father, The Prince of Peace.

—Isaiah 9:4, 6

CONFUSED

If any of you lack wisdom, let him ask of God, that gives to all men liberally, and upbraids not; and it shall be given him.

—James 1:5

Good and upright is the Lord: therefore will He teach sinners in the way. The meek will He guide in judgment: and the meek will He teach His way.

—Psalm 25:8–9

But let him ask in faith, nothing wavering. For he that wavers is like a wave of the sea driven with the wind and tossed. For let not that man think that he shall receive any thing of the Lord. A double minded man is unstable in all his ways.

—James 1:6–8

For My thoughts are not your thoughts, neither are your ways My ways, says the LORD*. For as the heavens are higher than the earth, so are My ways higher than your ways, and My thoughts than your thoughts.*

—Isaiah 55:8–9

God is not the author of confusion,

but of peace.

—1 Corinthians 14:33

DEPRESSED

My soul melts for heaviness: strengthen You me according to Your word.

—Psalm 119:28

The LORD also will be a refuge for the oppressed, a refuge in times of trouble. And they that know Your name will put their trust in You: for You, LORD, have not forsaken them that seek you.

—Psalm 9:9–10

Why are you cast down, O my soul?
and why are you disquieted within me?
hope in God: for I shall yet praise Him,
who is the health of my countenance,
and my God.

—Psalm 43:5

My flesh and my heart fails:
but God is the strength of my heart,
and my portion for ever.
—Psalm 73:26

He brought me up also out of a horrible pit, out of the miry clay, and set my feet upon a rock, and established my goings.

—Psalm 40:2

This day is holy to our Lord: neither be you sorry; for the joy of the Lord is your strength....Hold your peace, for the day is holy; neither be you grieved.

—Nehemiah 8:10–11

DISAPPOINTED

Without counsel purposes are disappointed: but in the multitude of counselors they are established.

—Proverbs 15:22

Our soul waits for the Lord: He is our help and our shield. For our heart shall rejoice in Him, because we have trusted in His holy name.
Let Your mercy, O Lord, be upon us, according as we hope in You.

—Psalm 33:20–22

We know that all things work together
for good to them that love God,
to them who are the called according to
His purpose.
—Romans 8:28

Trust in Him at all times; you people,
pour out your heart before Him:
God is a refuge for us.
—Psalm 62:8

Verily God has heard me; He has
attended to the voice of my prayer.
Blessed be God, which has not turned
away my prayer,
nor His mercy from me.
—Psalm 66:19–20

FORSAKEN

For the Lord loves judgment,

and forsakes not His saints;

they are preserved for ever.

—Psalm 37:28

They that know Your name will put their trust in You: for You, Lord, have not forsaken them that seek you.

—Psalm 9:10

He has said, I will never leave you,

nor forsake you.

—Hebrews 13:5

I have been young, and now am old; yet have I not seen the righteous forsaken.

—Psalm 37:25

Be strong and of good courage, and do it: fear not, nor be dismayed: for the L*ORD* *God, even my God, will be with you; He will not fail you, nor forsake you.*

— 1 Chronicles 28:20

GUILTY

Blessed is he whose transgression is forgiven, whose sin is covered.
Blessed is the man to whom the Lord
imputes not iniquity,
and in whose spirit there is no guile.

—Psalm 32:1–2

There is therefore now no condemnation to them which are in Christ Jesus, who walk not after the flesh, but after the Spirit. For the law of the Spirit of life in Christ Jesus has made me free from the law of sin and death.

—Romans 8:1–2

All have sinned, and come short of the glory of God; being justified freely by His grace through the redemption that is in Christ Jesus.

—Romans 3:23–24

Be it known to you therefore, men and brethren, that through this man is preached to you the forgiveness of sins: and by Him all that believe are justified from all things.

—Acts 13:38–39

The blood of Christ, who through the eternal Spirit offered Himself without spot to God, [shall] *purge your conscience from dead works to serve the living God.*

—Hebrews 9:14

HELPLESS

For I the Lord *your God will*
hold your right hand, saying to you,
Fear not; I will help you.
—Isaiah 41:13

Behold, God is my helper: the Lord is with them that uphold my soul.

—Psalm 54:4

You have seen it;
for You behold mischief and spite...
You are the helper of the fatherless.
—Psalm 10:14

So that we may boldly say, The Lord is my helper, and I will not fear what man shall do to me.

—Hebrews 13:6

Likewise the Spirit also helps our infirmities: for we know not what we should pray for as we ought: but the Spirit Itself makes intercession for us with groanings which cannot be uttered.

—Romans 8:26

IMPATIENT

Wait on the Lord*: be of good courage,*
and He shall strengthen your heart:
wait, I say, on the Lord*.*
—Psalm 27:14

We glory in tribulations also:
knowing that tribulation works patience;
and patience, experience;
and experience, hope.
—Romans 5:3–4

Rest in the Lord,

and wait patiently for him.

—Psalm 37:7

The trying of your faith works patience.
But let patience have her perfect work,
that you may be perfect and entire,
wanting nothing.
—James 1:3–4

Wait on the Lord, and keep His way,
and He shall exalt you to
inherit the land.
—Psalm 37:34

LONELY

Lo, I am with you always, even to the end of the world.

—Matthew 28:20

I will not leave you comfortless: I will come to you. Yet a little while, and the world sees Me no more; but you see Me: because I live, you shall live also.

—John 14:18–19

He has said, I will never leave you,

nor forsake you.

—Hebrews 13:5

When my father and my mother forsake me, then the L*ORD* *will take me up.*

—Psalm 27:10

When you pass through the waters,

I will be with you.

—Isaiah 43:2

WORRIED

Be [anxious] *for nothing; but in every thing by prayer and supplication with thanksgiving let your requests be made known to God. And the peace of God, which passes all understanding, shall keep your hearts and minds through Christ Jesus.*

—Philippians 4:6–7

Take no thought, saying, What shall we eat? or, What shall we drink? or, Wherewithal shall we be clothed?... For your heavenly Father knows that you have need of all these things. But seek you first the kingdom of God, and His righteousness; and all these things shall be added to you.

—Matthew 6:31–33

Which of you [by worrying] *can add to his stature one cubit? If you then be not able to do that thing which is least, why take you thought for the rest?*

—Luke 12:25–26

Humble yourselves therefore under the mighty hand of God, that He may exalt you in due time: casting all your care upon Him; for He cares for you.

—1 Peter 5:6–7

Take therefore no thought for the morrow: for the morrow shall take thought for the things of itself.

—Matthew 6:34

GOD'S PROMISES IN TIMES OF...

DOUBT

Be strong and of a good courage;
be not afraid, neither be you dismayed:
for the Lord *your God is with you*
wherever you go.

—Joshua 1:9

Faith is the substance of things hoped for,
the evidence of things not seen.
—Hebrews 11:1

And Jesus answering said to them, Have faith in God. For verily I say to you, That whosoever shall say to this mountain, Be you removed, and be you cast into the sea; and shall not doubt in his heart, but shall believe that those things which he says shall come to pass; he shall have whatsoever he says.

—Mark 11:22–23

Whatsoever you shall ask in prayer,

believing, you shall receive.

—Matthew 21:22

In the multitude of my thoughts within me Your comforts delight my soul.

—Psalm 94:19

TROUBLE

God is our refuge and strength, a very present help in trouble.

—Psalm 46:1

The salvation of the righteous is of the LORD: He is their strength in the time of trouble. And the LORD shall help them, and deliver them: He shall deliver them from the wicked, and save them, because they trust in him.

—Psalm 37:39–40

These things I have spoken to you, that in Me you might have peace. In the world you shall have tribulation: but be of good cheer; I have overcome the world.

—John 16:33

Many are the afflictions of the righteous:
but the Lord *delivers him out*
of them all.

—Psalm 34:19

Because he has set his love upon Me,
therefore will I deliver him:
I will set him on high, because he has
known My name. He shall call upon
Me, and I will answer him:
I will be with him in trouble; I will
deliver him, and honor him.

—Psalm 91:14–15

TEMPTATION

There has no temptation taken you but such as is common to man: but God is faithful, who will not suffer you to be tempted above that you are able; but will with the temptation also make a way to escape, that you may be able to bear it.

—1 Corinthians 10:13

Blessed is the man that endures temptation: for when he is tried, he shall receive the crown of life, which the Lord has promised to them that love Him.

—James 1:12

For we have not a high priest which cannot be touched with the feeling of our infirmities; but was in all points tempted like as we are, yet without sin. Let us therefore come boldly to the throne of grace, that we may obtain mercy, and find grace to help in time of need.

—Hebrews 4:15–16

[God] *delivered just Lot, vexed with the filthy conversation of the wicked…the Lord knows how to deliver the godly out of temptations, and to reserve the unjust unto the day of judgment to be punished.*

—2 Peter 2:7, 9

Abstain from all appearance of evil. And the very God of peace sanctify you wholly; and I pray God your whole spirit and soul and body be preserved blameless to the coming of our Lord Jesus Christ. Faithful is He that calls you, who also will do it.

—1 Thessalonians 5:22–24

SATANIC ATTACK

Wherefore take to you the whole armor of God, that you may be able to withstand in the evil day, and having done all, to stand.

—Ephesians 6:13

Submit yourselves therefore to God.

Resist the devil,

and he will flee from you.

—James 4:7

The God of peace shall bruise Satan under your feet shortly. The grace of our Lord Jesus Christ be with you.

—Romans 16:20

Our Lord Jesus Christ…gave Himself for our sins, that He might deliver us from this present evil world, according to the will of God and our Father.

—Galatians 1:3–4

I pray not that You should take them out of the world, but that You should keep them from the evil. They are not of the world, even as I am not of the world.

—John 17:15–16

TRIAL

Blessed is the man that endures temptation: for when he is tried, he shall receive the crown of life, which the Lord has promised to them that love Him.

—James 1:12

[You] *are kept by the power of God through faith to salvation ready to be revealed in the last time. Wherein you greatly rejoice, though now for a season, if need be, you are in heaviness through manifold temptations: that the trial of your faith, being much more precious than of gold that perishes, though it be tried with fire, might be found to praise and honor and glory at the appearing of Jesus Christ.*

—1 Peter 1:5–7

We glory in tribulations also: knowing that tribulation works patience.

—Romans 5:3

My brethren, count it all joy when you fall into divers temptations; knowing this, that the trying of your faith works patience. But let patience have her perfect work, that you may be perfect and entire, wanting nothing.

—James 1:2–4

SICKNESS

The LORD will take away from
you all sickness, and will put none of the
evil diseases of Egypt,
which you know, upon you.
—Deuteronomy 7:15

Is any sick among you? let him call for the elders of the church; and let them pray over him, anointing him with oil in the name of the Lord: and the prayer of faith shall save the sick, and the Lord shall raise him up.

—James 5:14–15

He cast out the spirits with His word, and healed all that were sick: that it might be fulfilled which was spoken by Isaiah the prophet, saying, Himself took our infirmities, and bore our sicknesses.

—Matthew 8:16–17

These signs shall follow them that believe…they shall lay hands on the sick, and they shall recover.

—Mark 16:17–18

I will take sickness away from the midst of you.

—Exodus 23:25

DEATH

I am persuaded, that neither death, nor life, nor angels, nor principalities, nor powers, nor things present, nor things to come…shall be able to separate us from the love of God, which is in Christ Jesus our Lord.

—Romans 8:38–39

In My Father's house are many mansions: if it were not so, I would have told you. I go to prepare a place for you. And if I go and prepare a place for you, I will come again, and receive you to Myself; that where I am, there you may be also.

—John 14:2–3

We are confident, I say, and willing rather to be absent from the body, and to be present with the Lord. Wherefore we labor, that, whether present or absent, we may be accepted of him.

—2 Corinthians 5:8–9

O death, where is your sting? O grave, where is your victory? The sting of death is sin; and the strength of sin is the law. But thanks be to God, which gives us the victory through our Lord Jesus Christ.

—1 Corinthians 15:55–57

Yea, though I walk through the valley of the shadow of death, I will fear no evil: for You are with me; Your rod and Your staff they comfort me.

—Psalm 23:4

SORROW

The Lord *has comforted His people,*
and will have mercy upon His afflicted.
—Isaiah 49:13

God shall wipe away all tears from their eyes; and there shall be no more death, neither sorrow, nor crying, neither shall there be any more pain: for the former things are passed away.

—Revelation 21:4

Blessed are they that mourn: for they shall be comforted.

—Matthew 5:4

They that sow in tears shall reap in joy.
He that goes forth and weeps,
bearing precious seed, shall doubtless
come again with rejoicing, bringing his
sheaves with him.
—Psalm 126:5–6

The redeemed of the LORD shall return, and come with singing to Zion; and everlasting joy shall be upon their head: they shall obtain gladness and joy; and sorrow and mourning shall flee away.

—Isaiah 51:11

BACKSLIDING

A voice was heard upon the high places, weeping and supplications of the children of Israel: for they have perverted their way, and they have forgotten the L*ORD* *their God. Return, you backsliding children, and I will heal your backslidings.*

—Jeremiah 3:21–22

I have blotted out, as a thick cloud, your transgressions, and, as a cloud, your sins: return to Me; for I have redeemed you.

—Isaiah 44:22

My little children, these things write I to you, that you sin not. And if any man sin, we have an advocate with the Father, Jesus Christ the righteous.

—1 John 2:1

*All we like sheep have gone astray;
we have turned every one to his own
way; and the LORD has laid on Him the
iniquity of us all.*

—Isaiah 53:6

Come now, and let us reason together, says the Lord: though your sins be as scarlet, they shall be as white as snow; though they be red like crimson, they shall be as wool.

—Isaiah 1:18

PERSONAL ATTACK

If God be for us, who can be against us?

—Romans 8:31

Let all those that put their trust in
You rejoice: let them ever shout for joy,
because You defend them.

—Psalm 5:11

They shall fight against you, but they shall not prevail against you: for I am with you to save you and to deliver you, says the LORD*. And I will deliver you out of the hand of the wicked, and I will redeem you out of the hand of the terrible.*

—Jeremiah 15:20–21

Fear you not, stand still,
and see the salvation of the LORD,
which He will show to you to day....
The LORD shall fight for you,
and you shall hold your peace.
—Exodus 14:13–14

The salvation of the righteous is of the Lord: He is their strength in the time of trouble. And the Lord shall help them, and deliver them: He shall deliver them from the wicked, and save them, because they trust in him.

—Psalm 37:39–40

PERSECUTION

Blessed are they which are persecuted

for righteousness' sake:

for theirs is the kingdom of heaven.

—Matthew 5:10

Love your enemies, bless them that curse you, do good to them that hate you, and pray for them which spitefully use you, and persecute you;
that you may be the children of your Father which is in heaven.
—Matthew 5:44–45

You shall be hated of all men for My name's sake. But there shall not a hair of your head perish. In your patience possess you your souls.

—Luke 21:17–19

Fear none of those things which you shall suffer: behold, the devil shall cast some of you into prison, that you may be tried... be you faithful to death, and I will give you a crown of life.

—Revelation 2:10

They shall lay their hands on you,

and persecute you....Settle it therefore in

your hearts, not to meditate before what

you shall answer:

for I will give you a mouth and wisdom,

which all your adversaries shall not be

able to gainsay nor resist.

—Luke 21:12, 14–15

We are troubled on every side, yet not distressed; we are perplexed, but not in despair; persecuted, but not forsaken; cast down, but not destroyed.

—2 Corinthians 4:8–9

GOD'S PROMISES FOR THOSE WHO...

SUFFER FOR CHRIST

If you be reproached for the name of Christ, happy are you; for the Spirit of glory and of God rests upon you.

—1 Peter 4:14

When you do well, and suffer for it, you take it patiently, this is acceptable with God.

—1 Peter 2:20

As you are partakers of the sufferings,
so shall you be also of the consolation.
—2 Corinthians 1:7

It is a faithful saying: For if we be dead with Him, we shall also live with Him.

—2 Timothy 2:11

[Your tribulations are] *a manifest token of the righteous judgment of God, that you may be counted worthy of the kingdom of God, for which you also suffer: seeing it is a righteous thing with God to recompense tribulation to them that trouble you.*

—2 Thessalonians 1:5–6

If so be that we suffer with Him, that we may be also glorified together. For I reckon that the sufferings of this present time are not worthy to be compared with the glory which shall be revealed in us.

—Romans 8:17–18

The God of all grace, who has called us to His eternal glory by Christ Jesus, after that you have suffered a while, make you perfect, stablish, strengthen, settle you.

—1 Peter 5:10